GRAPHIC LIBRARY

GRAPHIC HISTORY

The BUFFALO SOLDIERS and the AMERICAN WEST

by Jason Glaser
illustrated by Tod Smith
and Charles Barnett III

Consultant:
Dr. Lois Brown
Mount Holyoke College
South Hadley, Massachusetts

Capstone press
Mankato, Minnesota

Graphic Library is published by Capstone Press,
1710 Roe Crest Drive, North Mankato, Minnesota 56003.
www.capstonepub.com

Printed in the United States of America in Stevens Point, Wisconsin.

072013
007585R

Library of Congress Cataloging-in-Publication Data

Glaser, Jason.

The Buffalo Soldiers and the American West / by Jason Glaser ; illustrated by Tod Smith and Charles Barnett III.

p. cm.—(Graphic library. Graphic history)

Includes bibliographical references and index.

ISBN-13: 978-0-7368-4966-1 (hardcover) ISBN-10: 0-7368-4966-1 (hardcover)

ISBN-13: 978-0-7368-6204-2 (softcover pbk.) ISBN-10: 0-7368-6204-8 (softcover pbk.)

1. African Americans—West (U.S.)—History—19th century—Juvenile literature. 2. African American soldiers—West (U.S.)—History—19th century—Juvenile literature. 3. United States. Army—African American troops—History—19th century—Juvenile literature. 4. Frontier and pioneer life—West (U.S.)—Juvenile literature. 5. Indians of North America—Wars—1866–1895—Juvenile literature. I. Smith, Tod, ill. II. Title. III. Series.

E185.925.G543 2006

978'.00496073—dc22 2005006527

Summary: In graphic novel format, tells the story of the African American soldiers known as Buffalo Soldiers, who fought against American Indians and protected the Western Frontier of the United States.

Art and Editorial Direction
Jason Knudson and Blake A. Hoena

Designer
Bob Lentz

Colorists
Bob Lentz and Kim Brown

Editor
Donald Lemke

Editor's note: Direct quotations from primary sources are indicated by a yellow background.

Direct quotations appear on the following pages:

Page 12 (commissioner), from PBS Online's *American Experience,* "Transcontinental Railroad" (http://www.pbs.org/wgbh/amex/tcrr/sfeature/sf_map_text_07.html).

Page 12, from Santanta's speech at Medicine Lodge, 1867, as quoted in Oklahoma Historical Society's *Chronicles of Oklahoma,* Volume 13, No. 1, March, 1935, "The Kiowa's Defiance" (http://digital.library.okstate.edu/Chronicles/v013/v013p030.html).

Page 24, from *African Americans on the Western Frontier* edited by Monroe Lee Billington and Roger D. Hardaway (Niwot: University Press of Colorado, 1998).

Page 26, from *American Patriots: The Story of Blacks in the Military from the Revolution to Desert Storm* by Gail Lumet Buckley (New York: Random House, 2001).

Page 27, from *My American Journey* by Colin Powell with Joseph E. Persico (New York: Random House, 1995).

TABLE OF CONTENTS

CHAPTER 1

Westward Expansion

In 1862, the U.S. Congress passed the Homestead Act. This law allowed settlers to buy cheap land in the western United States. Soon, thousands of Americans journeyed onto the prairies of the Great Plains.

American Indian tribes had lived throughout the Western Frontier for hundreds of years.
Every day, more white people come here. They build roads, houses, and chase away the buffalo.
Without the buffalo, our families starve.
We must do something!
Over the next few years, some Indians tried to scare the white settlers away.
Run, Emily!
Run!

We're not safe here, John.
I know, Emily. The government should do something about these attacks.
In 1866, the U.S. Army had few soldiers to protect western settlers. Most troops had just finished fighting the Civil War (1861–1865), including about 200,000 African Americans.
We can't expect white soldiers to serve any longer, gentlemen. Why don't we send black troops out West?
Just because we let them fight during the Civil War, doesn't mean we should use them again.
Why not? They have earned their freedom and the right to fight.
The Civil War helped end slavery in the United States but didn't stop unfair treatment of African Americans.

In July 1866, Congress formed African American military units to protect the American West. Some were horseback divisions called cavalry. Others were infantry divisions that would fight on foot.
JOIN THE ARMY
What does that sign say?
If you enlist, we'll teach you how to read. And we'll pay you for it!
That's the best offer you boys are going to get.
Maybe he's right.
With few chances for work or education, many African Americans decided to join. In the first year, almost 2,000 signed up to fight on horseback. They formed nearly 20 percent of the total U.S. cavalry.

The army had plenty of volunteers but few supplies. Uniforms, guns, horses, and other equipment were old or worn out.
Giddyap!
That old horse is as useless as this leaky canteen.
Yeah, and this busted gun.
The army also needed officers to lead the new divisions. African Americans weren't allowed to become officers. Many whites refused to help, including Lieutenant Colonel George Armstrong Custer.
The army wants you to lead one of the new black units, Lieutenant Custer.
I'd rather quit than lead a bunch of black troops into battle. Everyone knows they can't follow orders.

Officers who did volunteer often made African American soldiers march for hours every day . . .
I bet they don't make the white soldiers work this hard.
I wouldn't care so much if we had better shoes.
. . . and severely punished their troops.
This will teach you to question my orders!
Poor treatment, food, and housing made many soldiers ill. Within a year, hundreds died from disease. Still, many refused to quit.
Someday we'll get the respect we deserve.

CHAPTER 2

Keeping Order

Although they had little experience, the young soldiers soon proved their bravery in battle.
These black soldiers don't give up. They are ferocious like the buffalo.
Their bravery in battle earned African Americans the respect of their enemies, including Cheyenne and Comanche Indians.
They also earned a nickname . . .
Why do the Indians keep calling us Buffalo Soldiers?
Probably because of our curly hair.
And our dark skin.
Well, at least they say it with respect. It's better than some things we've been called by white men.

In October, President Andrew Johnson formed the Indian Peace Commission. This group met with Cheyenne, Kiowa, Apache, Comanche, and Arapaho leaders in Kansas.
I have heard you intend to settle us on a reservation near the mountains.
Yes. We plan to build a railroad through these lands.
I don't want to settle.
You cannot stop the locomotive any more than you can stop the sun or the moon.
After the talks, some groups agreed to move to the reservations.
It appears we have no choice, Santanta.
Others refused to go peacefully.
I will not leave this land. I will fight until we are free.

Over the next few years, the U.S. government made treaties with Indian tribes on the Western Frontier. Many Buffalo Soldiers built and guarded forts near the reservations.
Heave!

During this time, members of the 10th Cavalry protected the building of the transcontinental railroad.
When we're finished, these tracks will stretch clear across the country.
Yeah, and right through Indian land.
Aren't you afraid of attacks?
That's why we keep these black soldiers around.
By 1870, the railroad brought more white settlers to the area. Soon, Buffalo Soldiers were ordered to protect reservations. They chased off homesteaders, called Boomers.
You can't stay here. This is Indian land.
I'm surprised they let a black man wear a uniform.

They also chased off white hunters who were killing buffalo by the thousands.
Stop!
As the buffalo die, so do our people.
The U.S. government hasn't given us the supplies they promised.
We must leave the reservations and search for food.

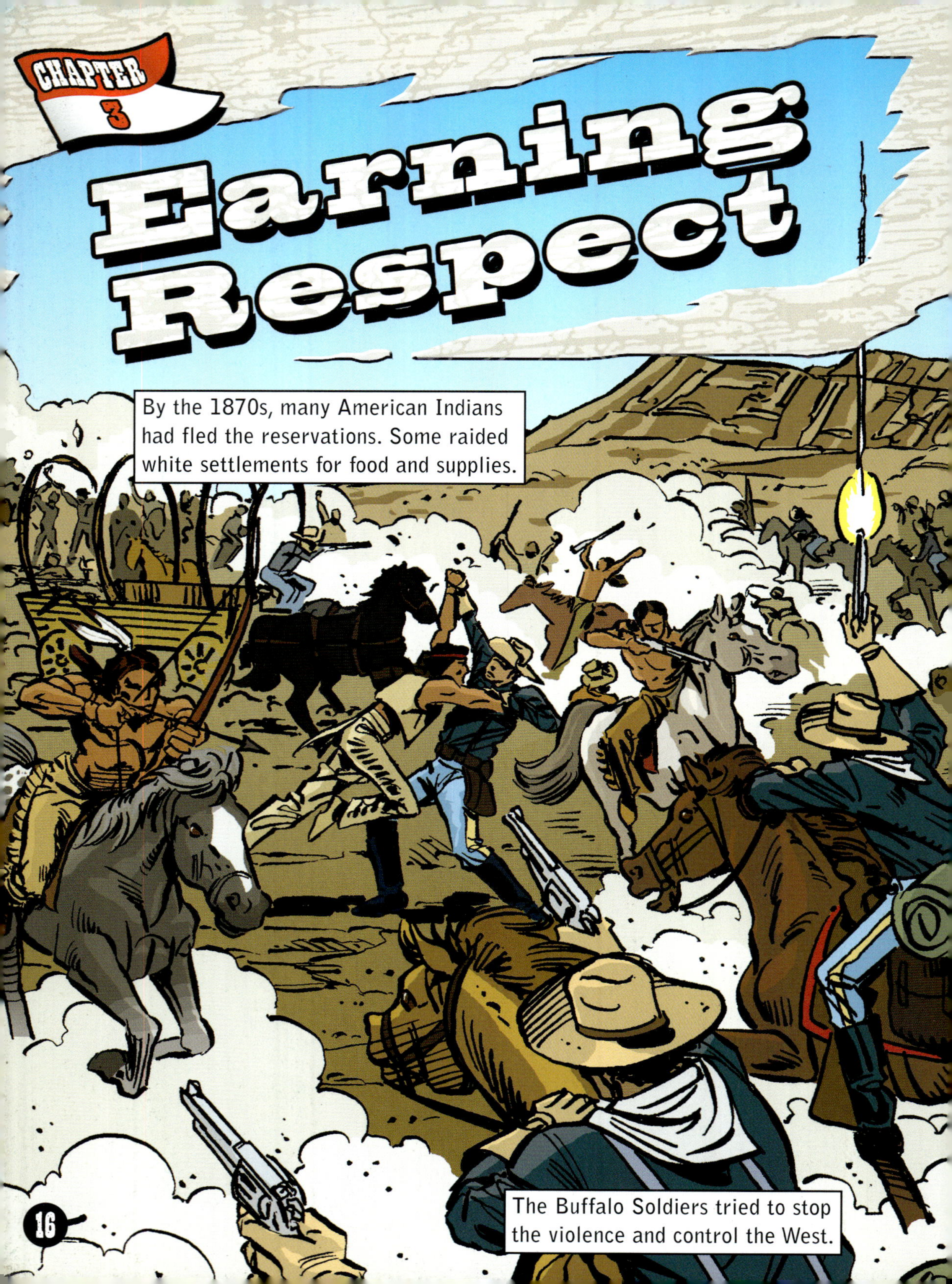

CHAPTER 3
Earning Respect
By the 1870s, many American Indians had fled the reservations. Some raided white settlements for food and supplies.
The Buffalo Soldiers tried to stop the violence and control the West.

They also stayed ready to assist other units.
The 7th Cavalry has been attacked!
They're trapped near an Indian camp!
Let's go, men!
Are you all right, General Custer?
I'm fine!
They surprised us a bit. It won't happen again.
Many of their rescues were never written down. Still, the Buffalo Soldiers became famous for showing up in the nick of time.

Over the next 10 years, units of Buffalo Soldiers were scattered across the American West.
They arrested outlaws on the prairies of the Great Plains . . .
. . . chased Mexican bandits through the deserts of the Southwest . . .
PACIFIC OCEAN
Ft. Thomas
Sierra

MINN.
MONT.
WYO.
COLO.
Colorado River
. . . delivered mail through frigid Midwest winters . . .
Ft. Larned
Mississippi River
MISS.
. . . and tracked Indian warriors under the heat of the Texas sun.
OF
MEXICO

For their efforts in the West, some Buffalo Soldiers received medals. Others were given greater responsibility. In 1877, Henry O. Flipper became the first African American officer of the Buffalo Soldiers.
New orders, men. We're joining the search for Victorio!
Yes sir, Lieutenant Flipper.
Victorio was an Apache leader who raided ranches and small towns in Texas for weapons and supplies.

One of Victorio's strengths was how fast his group traveled.
I can get him, Lieutenant Flipper!
He's made it back into Mexico. We're not allowed to chase him there.
How did they find me again?

The leaders of Mexico also wanted to catch Victorio. In 1880, they allowed the 10th Cavalry into their country.
Victorio was not able to get back into the United States.

After fighting bravely, he was killed by Mexican troops on October 15, 1880.

Like Victorio, other American Indian leaders fought to save their land and way of life. By the late 1800s, many of them had surrendered or been killed.
Sitting Bull
Roman Nose
Crazy Horse
In 1886, Geronimo became the last American Indian warrior to surrender.
Once I moved about like the wind. Now I surrender to you and that is all.

CHAPTER 4
Beyond the Frontier

Meanwhile, Cuba tried to declare independence from Spain. The United States sent Navy ships to protect their shipments near Cuba. On February 15, 1898, the USS *Maine* exploded.
BOOM!!
USS MAINE
The U.S. government believed Spain planted a mine that sank the ship.
Many Buffalo Soldiers were sent overseas for the first time.
We're headed to Cuba for a fight against Spain!
Maybe this time the army will see that we truly belong.

They fought beside Theodore Roosevelt, leader of the Rough Riders. Roosevelt later became president.
No one can tell whether it was the Rough Riders or the men of the Buffalo Soldiers who came forward with the greater courage.
After the Spanish-American War (1898), Buffalo Soldiers fought bravely in World War II (1939–1945). During the Korean War (1950–1953), the U.S. military desegregated. African American soldiers were no longer separate from white soldiers.

In 1989, Colin Powell became the first African American chairman of the Joint Chiefs of Staff. This is the highest post in the military.
In 1990, Powell started the construction of a memorial to the Buffalo Soldiers at Fort Leavenworth, Kansas.
O SOLDIERS
Since 1641, there has never been a time in this country when blacks were unwilling to serve and sacrifice for America.

MORE ABOUT BUFFALO SOLDIERS

- Congress originally formed six African American military units in 1866. They included the 9th and 10th Cavalry and 38th, 39th, 40th, and 41st Infantry. Three years later, the infantry units combined to form the 24th and 25th Infantry.

- While serving in the army, Buffalo Soldiers earned $13 a month plus food, clothing, and shelter. Although the pay was low, it equaled the amount received by white troops.

- Before 1948, women were not allowed to join the army. In November 1866, an African American woman named Cathay Williams disguised herself as a man and signed up. She became the first and only female Buffalo Soldier. During her two years of service, she called herself William Cathay.

- Buffalo Soldiers tested new equipment for the military. During the 1890s, the U.S. Army wanted to replace horses with bicycles. In 1897, Buffalo Soldiers known as the 25th Infantry Bicycle Corps rode bicycles 1,900 miles from Missoula, Montana, to St. Louis, Missouri. They were the Army's only bicycle unit.

- Buffalo Soldiers chased well-known outlaws throughout the Wild West. Some of these infamous men were William "Billy the Kid" Bonney and Francisco "Pancho" Villa.

- In 1870, Emmanuel Stance became the first Buffalo Soldier to receive the Medal of Honor. This honor is the highest award for courage given by the U.S. military. Seventeen other Buffalo Soldiers received the award for bravery in the West.

- In 1877, 21-year-old Henry O. Flipper became the first African American to graduate from West Point. His military education helped Flipper become the first African American officer in the United States.

- In 2004, the 10th Cavalry, still known as the Buffalo Soldiers, fought during Operation Iraqi Freedom. Unlike the original Buffalo Soldiers, this unit had both African American and white troops. They were led by Lieutenant Colonel Reginald Allen, the first African American to command the Buffalo Soldiers in combat.

GLOSSARY

Congress (KONG-griss)—the branch of the U.S. government that makes laws

enlist (en-LIST)—to join the army, navy, or one of the other armed forces

frontier (fruhn-TEER)—the unsettled territories of western North America in the 1800s

lieutenant (loo-TEN-ant)—the first rank of officer in the military; officers are ranked higher than regular soldiers.

reservation (rez-er-VAY-shuhn)—an area of land set aside by the U.S. government for American Indians

settlement (SET-uhl-muhnt)—a group of buildings and the people living in them

INTERNET SITES

FactHound offers a safe, fun way to find Internet sites related to this book. All of the sites on FactHound have been researched by our staff.

Here's how:

1. *Visit www.facthound.com*
2. Type in this special code **0736849661** for age-appropriate sites. Or enter a search word related to this book for a more general search.
3. Click on the **Fetch It** button.

FactHound will fetch the best sites for you!

READ MORE

Barnett, Tracy. *The Buffalo Soldiers.* The American West. Broomall, Penn.: Mason Crest, 2003.

Clinton, Catherine. *The Black Soldier: 1492 to the Present.* Boston: Houghton Mifflin, 2000.

Flanagan, Alice K. *The Buffalo Soldiers.* We the People. Minneapolis, Minn.: Compass Point Books, 2005.

Halpern, Monica. *Railroad Fever: Building the Transcontinental Railroad, 1830–1870.* Crossroads America. Washington, DC: National Geographic, 2004.

Raabe, Emily. *Buffalo Soldiers and the Western Frontier.* Westward Ho! New York: PowerKids Press, 2003.

BIBLIOGRAPHY

Buckley, Gail Lumet. *American Patriots: The Story of Blacks in the Military from the Revolution to Desert Storm.* New York: Random House, 2001.

Powell, Colin, with Joseph E. Persico. *My American Journey.* New York: Random House, 1995.

"Transcontinental Railroad." *American Experience.* PBS Online. http://www.pbs.org/wgbh/amex/tcrr/sfeature/sf_map_text_07.html

INDEX